ARNOLD COOKE

SONATA IN B FLAT

for Clarinet and Piano

Order No: NOV 120130

NOVELLO PUBLISHING LIMITED
8/9 Frith Street, London W1V 5TZ

Written for the Hampton Music Club

Time of performance about 20 minutes

A recording of this work will be available in the Autumn of 1982 on Hyperion A 66044. (Thea King—clarinet, Clifford Benson—piano).

Sonata in B flat
for Clarinet and Piano

I

ARNOLD COOKE
1959

II

III

48

cresc.

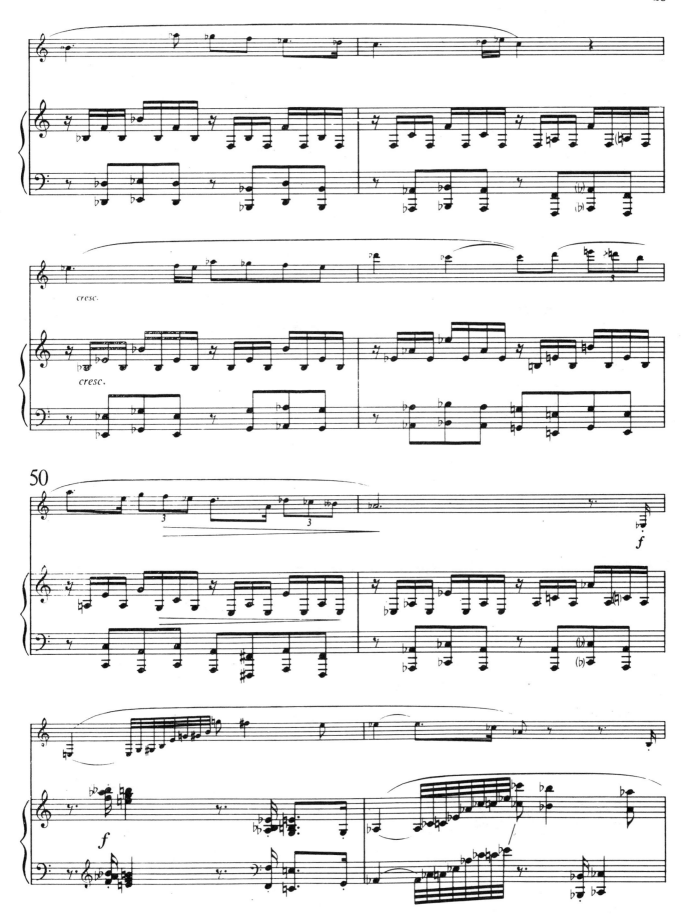

IV

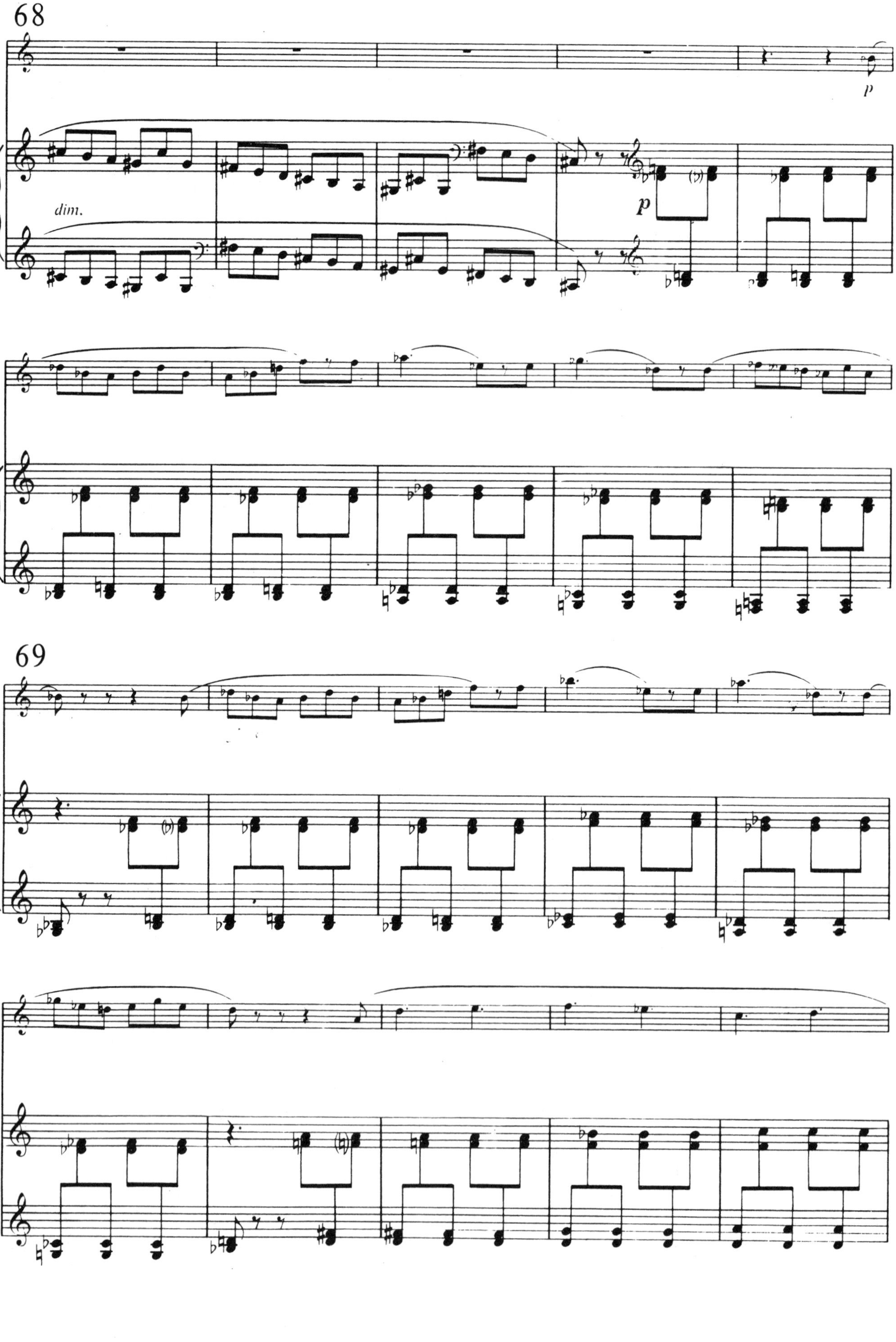
68
p
dim.
p
69

allargando

Printed in Great Britain by Headway Press Ltd

MUSIC FOR CLARINET

SOLO

BENNETT, Richard Rodney
SCENA III
SONATINA

BLAKE, David
ARIAS

MANDUELL, John
PRAYERS FROM THE ARK

CLARINET & PIANO

BLISS, Arthur
PASTORAL FOR CLARINET & PIANO

CAMILLERI, Charles
DIVERTIMENTO

COOKE, Arnold
CLARINET CONCERTO
SONATA IN B FLAT

DEBUSSY, Claude
A DEBUSSY CLARINET ALBUM

ELGAR, Edward
AN ELGAR CLARINET ALBUM

FASCH, Johann
ed Richard Platt
CONCERTO IN B FLAT

FAURE, Gabriel
A FAURE CLARINET ALBUM

HARVEY, Jonathan
TRANSFORMATIONS OF 'LOVE BADE
ME WELCOME'

HOROVITZ, Joseph
SONATINA

JACOB, Gordon
SONATINA

LAWTON, Sidney
FUGUE ON A NURSERY THEME

McCABE, John
THREE PIECES

MORLEY, Angela
FOUR CHARACTERS

SATIE, Erik
A SATIE CLARINET ALBUM

STEEL, Christopher
SONATINA

TCHAIKOVSKY, Peter
A TCHAIKOVSKY CLARINET ALBUM

WAGNER, Richard
A WAGNER CLARINET ALBUM

606 (90)